CIE BUSES IN THE 1970s & 80s – SINGLE DECKERS

Leabharlanna Poibli Chathair Bhaile Átha Cliath
Dublin City Public Libraries

Former P164, a Leyland Tiger OPS3/1 was a creditable thirty two years old when this photograph was taken at Parnell Place Bus Station in Cork. Built by CIÉ at Spa Road as a 30-seater coach front entrance coach for the fledgling coach tour business in 1950. Appropriately named The Lee, it was was converted to a towing vehicle in 1971 and is now preserved as such.

P318, one of the narrower 2.3m Leyland PS2/14s, and dating from June 1953 was also converted to recovery duties. It is seen in a dejected state at the Coal Quay in Sligo from which garage it served as their tow car. It was acquired in January 1986 by the West of Ireland Steam Railway Association as a donor vehicle for other preserved buses and coaches of its class and was eventually scrapped for spares.

CIE's first foray into the world of the underfloor-engined vehicle was a fleet of 88 Leyland PSU1 Royal Tigers built between 1954 and 1955. The U class, known colloquially as the U Boats, featured 50 C34C coaches (called Banana Boats – see page 7) followed by 38 1 and 2 door buses. Some of the class went on to become driver training vehicles in which guise U78 is seen withdrawn in Broadstone Garage in May 1979 prior to its rescue by the Transport Museum Society of Ireland and currently awaits restoration.

The success of the underfloor engine bus and the closure of many branch lines on the railway led CIÉ to order 170 Leyland L2 chassis with rugged and utilitarian 45 seater bodies which were constructed at Spa Road Works between 1961 and 1965. E18 entered service in December 1961 and became a driver trainer in May 1978, finally being withdrawn in October 1993 when it was bought for preservation after almost thirty two years service.

The E class was to become the backbone of rural services in the early 1960s with many of the class lasting in service for over twenty years. E67 was new in April 1962 and became a driver trainer in Cork in February 1980 where is it photographed. It was broken up on site in Capwell in 1991.

A line up of driver training vehicles in Broadstone in June 1978 show from left: E31, which became a driver trainer for Iarnród Eireann, E44 and U10 a "banana boat" dating from 1955 and awaits restoration by the Transport Museum Society of Ireland.

Following regular service, many Es ended up as school buses and redesignated SE. SE88 is seen in Dundalk Garage painted in the standard school bus livery of primrose yellow and white.

Another version of the school bus livery is seen on SE92, also in Dundalk.

E109, at this stage based in Dundalk is seen at the former Witham Street Transport Museum in Belfast on an enthusiasts' special prior to its redesignation as SE109 and transfer to the schools fleet.

Lower Knox Street in Sligo is the setting for this photograph of E124 taken in May 1982. The bus had been in a bad collision in 1974 when it was sandwiched between M97 and M114 and was finally withdrawn in 1984.

Donegal was the last bastion for regular services of Es. Their rugged construction made them ideal for the then often torturous roads in the county. E140 heads towards the Bus Station in Letterkenny from the town centre in May 1979. It became a driver trainer in 1985 and was acquired for preservation two years later. It was used in the Neil Jordan film Breakfast on Pluto produced in 2005.

Loading in Ballybofey, Co. Donegal is E147 *en route* to Strabane in April 1981. The destination blind on this vehicle is non-standard and most likely originated with the County Donegal Railways from whom CIÉ took over bus operations in 1971.

E151, then based in Waterford carries another popular transport advertisement, that of the now sadly defunct Pagoda Tea. The location of this August 1982 photograph is Waterford Station with its unique signal box in the background. The bus had been transferred from Ballina in 1982, where it had spent most of its working life, and did not last long in Waterford.

Another photograph from Ballybofey in April 1981 as E153 loads for Glenties with Stranlorlar based M14 in the background and a CIÉ GM-powered BTM tractor and trailer delivering beer to the left.

Some of the E class served with the Londonderry and Lough Swilly Railway Co, and former E160 as that company's fleet no. 209, is seen heading to Letterkenny via Burt in June 1982.

Another variation of the schoolbus livery applied by Dundalk Garage is seen on SE161. Usually out-stationed in remote areas, the bus was photographed in the garage during the 1981 school holidays and was withdrawn the following year.

Former E162 was converted for towing duties by Broadstone Garage in October 1981, becoming RV1 in the process. This was not generally perceived as having been a success however, and the Garage soon reverted to using Bedford and Leyland tractor units for towing and recovery. RV1 is seen in the Glen of the Downs in County Wicklow in the winter of 1982.

E166 having operated a special service into Derry City is seen laying over at the Bus Station at the Guildhall in February 1982. The bus would later pass to the Londonderry and Lough Swilly Railway Co in 1985 for spare parts.

The last of the 170 Es is seen at Broadstone in pristine condition in 1979. It and sister vehicle E169 were late into service in January 1965, over three years after the first of the class appeared. It became school bus SE170 in 1981 and passed into preservation with the Transport Museum Society of Ireland in 1985.

The experience of the L2s persuaded CIÉ to purchase more under-floor Leopards, and in April 1965 the first of the 270-strong David Ogle designed C Class PSU3/4Rs with CIÉ built bodies on frames by Metal Sections Ltd, rolled off the Spa Road production line. C5, an early example of the first batch of C1-C14, is seen at the former Waterford Bus Station in the Railway Station in March 1981. It still carried its distinctive front domes, most of the class having them replaced on overhaul.

High C – C20 has its chassis attended to in the chassis wash in Limerick Garage. The bus was based for much of its life in Limerick and was withdrawn in 1985 against a then large intake of KR class rural buses.

Vehicles in the series C1 – 190 were 9m long examples, whilst C191-270 were 11m long. C23, a 9m model is seen here working the arduous Cork - Ballina service is photographed at Galway Station in January 1984, showing a useful array of intermediate destinations. The bus had been quickly pressed into service on the day at Ennis as a result of the door on MG204, which it replaced, parting company with the vehicle in high winds. *Photo: Natalie Gardner*

The inside of Cs, in this case C23 at Ennis, tended to be claustrophobic with no opening windows, and a forced air ventilation system that was rarely effective. Despite this, the 270 vehicles in the class served a number of functions and were the backbone of the transport system in the 1970s. *Photo: Natalie Gardner*

C30 in Tralee sports an interesting modification – that of lower front panels from a D class Atlantean in this photograph taken in the depot in the summer of 1980.

Capwell in Cork is the location of this photograph of C45. Having entered service in July 1965, the bus entered the schools fleet as CS45 in January 1986 and was finally withdrawn in November 1992 having given 27 years service. It is believed to be preserved.

Rush hour in Shannon. C66 awaits passengers for Kildysart outside the Bombardier factory at Shannon Airport in May 1981.

Donnybrook's C82 and C85 in Dublin's Hawkins Street in March 1981. C82 has arrived from Sandymount on route 52, which replicated, in a large part, the route of the first horse-drawn tram in Dublin until its demise in the mid 1980s. The 52 bus route commenced operation in 1936, though the same route had run as the 44A commencing in June 1932. C85 waits for its next duty on route 47 to Rockbrook in the Dublin Mountains, popular with scouts and hikers, now also sadly discontinued.

Another Donnybrook C, C89 also in the then standard fleet livery of mid-buff lays over in Poolbeg Street opposite the loading bay for the Irish Press, then a hive of activity. The former Tara Street baths is also visible to the rear.

C74, new in September 1965 as a 45-seater bus was one of a batch of C71-76 inclusive along with C78 and C79 that were reconfigured to 41-seater coaches and allocated to Summerhill Garage for use on the Airport Express service. It later transferred to Donnybrook Garage, and then to Donegal where it is photographed in its last days of service in 1985, and was scrapped in August the following year.

An evocative shot of C124 on Dublin's Pearse Street having arrived on route 63 from Glenamuck.

C152 rests up at the popular sea-side village of Strandhill before returning to Sligo in February 1980. It became a school bus as CS152 in 1985 following replacement by KR class rural buses and was withdrawn in 1994.

Another Sligo vehicle, C155 receives valeting at the bus garage in the town. The bus survives at the Dromod narrow gauge railway in Co. Leitrim.

C188, one of 16 Cs to be based in Clontarf Garage awaits passengers at the Beresford Place terminus of route 53 to Alexandra Road in Dublin Port. Liberty Hall, Dublin's tallest building is due to be redeveloped, and with this the total streetscape will see a complete transformation. The bus stops in this photograph now facilitate the 103 and 105 Bus Éireann services to Ashbourne and Ratoath Co. Meath respectively.

Where as C1-190 were B45F buses, C191-270 were longer serving as B53F buses and C40F coaches. A recently out-shopped C194 photographed in Dundalk shows how visually pleasing these buses could be when freshly painted.

C203 heads towards Kilbarry in Waterford across the former John Redmond Bridge in the city in February 1980. A new bascule bridge was constructed on the site between 1982 to 1986 at a cost of almost IR£8m. The bus was converted to a dual door configuration as HB203 in April 1984 along with C254 at a later date for use as harbour buses for Rosslare Europort.

C231, with original domes at Busáras, Dublin's main provincial bus station, prepares to leave for Kildare in July 1984. This bus entered service as a 53 seat bus in April 1966, later to be converted to a 45 seat coach in 1968, and finally to a 55 seat bus in which format it was withdrawn in November 1985. It is currently preserved by the Transport Museum Society of Ireland.

C254 is seen on the Quays in Waterford in the summer of 1984 before it was converted to a dual-door 38 seat Harbour Bus for Rosslare Europort as HB254.

C258, photographed at Ballinasloe Railway Station in Co. Galway passed into preservation in November 1985 after almost 20 years service. It is restored in the red/cream livery.

C260 is seen at Sligo Railway Station in the brown and cream coach livery which it wore from new in September 1966. The bus was also acquired for preservation upon withdrawal in 1985 but subsequently scrapped. It was one of the five vehicles in the batch C256-260 that carried UZH registrations, the previous batch of C1-255 all being registered EZH, and the last, C261-270, being NZL.

C264, one of the last of the class to enter service in April 1968 is photographed beside the Harp Brewery in Dundalk. Of the 270 buses built, some 23 are in preservation.

In 1980, the first of 20 Van Hool bodied Bedford coaches arrived on hire from Doig's Coaches of Glasgow for tours service. Registered in the UK as CBC1T to CBC20T they subsequently received Irish registrations 21-40 HZJ. DVH8, in a line up with similar vehicles, is seen at the RDS in May 1981 carrying the registration 28 HZJ.

The second batch of Leyland Leopard PSU3A/4R coaches with Plaxton Panorama Elite bodies arrived in April 1969 for tours duties. With buses in short supply in the pre-Bombardier days, many coaches were converted to dual-purpose function throughout the country as a stop-gap measure. Waterford's PL21 was such a case, having been upgraded from a 44-seater coach when new in April 1969 to a 53-seater with bus seats in 1982.

PL33, in the livery as originally delivered, was also converted to a 53 seater dual-purpose vehicle and allocated to Dundalk Garage. It is seen in the Market Square in the town on the Fatima Park service.

WVH 14, a Leyland Worldmaster seen here at Waterford Railway Station started life in 1964 as WT15 with a CIÉ built coach body designed by the renowned David Ogle design agency, who were also responsible for the C class Leopards and D class Atlanteans. In 1970 it was rebodied with Van Hool Vistadome bodywork and lasted in service until 1985.

WVH20, also a rebodied Van Hool is seen in a variant of the coach livery in Roscrea, Co. Tipperary on an enthusiasts' special in January 1982.

LVH34 in Dundalk in May 1981, entered service in September 1963 as ET1, a Leyland PSU3/4R 40 seat coach. It was rebodied in April 1971 with this Van Hool 44-seat body and remained in the schools fleet as LVHS34 until 1992 when it was sold for scrap, having given over thirty years service.

LVH42, formerly ET9, was painted in the "Bombardier" coach livery in which it is seen in Capwell Garage, Cork.

In May 1971, the first of what would eventually become a fleet of 213-strong 12m Leyland Leopard PSU5/4Rs entered service as the M Class. It is believed that the first batch of these included the first chassis of its type, number 902056 as fleet number M30. On a summers evening in 1979, M7 in coach livery loads in Limerick on what today would be Bus Éireann's 051 Cork – Ballina service.

M8, also in coach colours was allocated to Donegal and was a regular on the Sligo-Derry service where it is seen in February 1979. It was latterly based in Stranorlar from where it was withdrawn as a school bus in 2000 after 29 years service.

A major programme to replace the Leyland engines in both D class Atlanteans and M class Leopards began in earnest in the late 1970s. CIÉ's inability to access much needed parts due to industrial upheaval at Leyland required to company to look elsewhere for power units for its vehicles. M15, re-engined MG15 in 1978 was one such vehicle and is seen in The Diamond in Donegal Town in March 1981.

Part of the re-engining programme saw some of the M class fitted with a DAF derivative of the Leyland .680 engine. MD35, which by this stage had been fitted with a DAF engine, is seen in Capwell Garage in Cork in the very attractive red and orange Expressway livery carried by some of the class. The vehicle had by then been fitted with an aluminium front, following a fire at the fibreglass moulding shop in Bus Maintenance Shops in Inchicore Railway Works. Cork however went to the trouble of getting new original fronts made for its allocation on Ms, and MD35 was later refitted with this.

MG48 with non-standard destination display is seen at Galway Railway Station in August 1984. The bus was cascaded into the school fleet operating around Longford. It was latterly allocated to Limerick for its last year of service, finally being retired in 1998 after some 27 years.

M87 in February 1981 in standard red and cream colours at Busaras in Dublin. Renumbered as a school bus MS87 in 1992, the bus also saw over 27 years in service being withdrawn from Dundalk in 1998 from where it was allocated in its later years.

MD103, allocated to Dundalk travels from the Garage to the town centre to take up duties. It was destroyed by fire in Dundalk Garage in 1990 along with M94.

Two views of the Carnew bus leaving Dublin city centre. MG112 turns onto Dublin's O'Connell Bridge from Eden Quay on a rainy February morning in 1982. At this stage the bus has received a General Motors 6V71 engine as part of the major refitting programme. The bus was acquired for preservation on withdrawal in 2001.

M115, also heads to Carnew on Dublin's George's Quay in March 1980. This bus was not included in the re-engining programme and retained its Leyland .680 engine, which probably explains its relatively early withdrawal in 1986 after a mere 14 years service. It was replaced by the last batch of KRs and was scrapped in Louth Commercials, Ardee, Co. Louth. Also worthy of note is the illuminated "Minimum Fare" sign which some of the class carried.

MD113 in Expressway livery applied to some of fleet arrives in Waterford from Cork. In the top left corner can be seen the old Bus Depot on the Quays, which is now a tourist office. The bus office moved to Waterford Railway Station until 2000, when a state-of-the-art facility on the Quay was opened.

M124 awaits departure from Busáras on the penultimate Edenderry bus of the night in early April 1980. The bus retained its Leyland running units throughout its life, though an experimental re-engining of six of the class, two each with Cummins, DAF and GM units was undertaken between 1975/6 and led to a major refit programme of almost two-thirds of the class with DAF and GM units from 1978 on, MC90 and MC167 being the only two Cummins examples.

M158 parked at Mullingar Railway Station, with M71 in the background in May 1982. Both vehicles would later join the schools fleet and redesignated MS158 and MS71 respectively.

MG185 arrives at Waterford Station from Limerick in June 1980. This was one of a batch downgraded from a coach 48 seater to a 55 dual purpose seater in 1986, eventually to become MGS185 in the schools fleet.

M192 outside Capwell Garage in Cork is seen on a service to Riverstick in May 1980. It was re-engined with a DAF unit as MD192 in January 1981.

MG196 on the Quay in Waterford was one of the last batch of 20 Ms designed as coaches, hence the lack of a destination display. In its latter days, as a school bus, MGS196 was re-seated to a staggering 61 bus-seat layout, but reverted to its dual-purpose 55 seater after a short while.

MG204 disgorges its passengers at Ennis Railway Station on the Cork – Ballina service in January 1984. It was this vehicle that C23 (page 23) took over from after its door blew off its mountings near Shannon Airport. The vehicle was involved in a serious accident in Gort Co. Galway the following October and withdrawn from service.

CIÉ's dissatisfaction with British Leyland, who had been up to then its main supplier of buses for over thirty years, came to a head in the late 1970's and a decision that a radically new design for a family of bus designs was required for the future. VanHool, then building the last of the D800 double deckers, plus some Volvo Ailsas for South Yorkshire PTE, produced a very attractive "Standee" high capacity city single decker, with a GM engine, and also a dual purpose rural /school bus based on the Bedford SB5 chassis, later to become vehicles in the SS771-800 series. However, VanHool's inability to sell buses overseas, other than the South Yorkshire batch, coupled with the reliance on dwindling CIÉ orders, inevitably led to the collapse of the Irish bus-building operation. Faced with this, CIÉ commissioned FFG Falkenried in Frankfurt to design and build six prototype buses - a 72 seat double decker, a 35 seat urban bus, two 47 seat rural buses, a 45 seat express/tour coach and a midibus suitable for wheelchair users. In 1978, the first of these prototypes arrived and was immediately boycotted by the unions. As V1, later to be designated KE1, it arrived in Dublin in 1979 and languished for some time under cover in Broadstone, before finally entering service in 1980. It is photographed in June 1981 in Waterford having arrived from Dublin.

KE4 was allocated to Limerick and is seen loading at the Railway Station there on a local service to Foynes in May 1983. This version of the maker's plate on the front of the vehicle was a rarity, most vehicles carrying only the Bombardier logo. It was withdrawn in 1996 and scrapped by Louth Commercials in Ardee in 2000.

Bill Kratz, Managing Director of Bombardier Ireland is photographed in June 1981 with an as yet undelivered KE8 along with the Transport Museum's 1953 Leyland PS2 P347 on an enthusiasts' visit to the plant.

First off Bombardier's production line in Shannon was a total of 51 express buses / coaches, all of which entered service in 1981. KE9, working the Dublin-Cork Expressway service, pauses at Cashel in May 1982, attracting some curious onlookers.

KE11 entered service on the Dublin – Letterkenny service in April 1981. It is seen at Busaras loading for Letterkenny in October 1982.

The rear of KE 17 prior to delivery at Bombardier in June 1981. It was allocated to Broadstone and operated the Dublin – Donegal Express.

Part of the production batch of KE2-51 included a series of coaches and KE22 is pictured at Busaras in May 1981 prior to departure on the Glendalough tour. As a coach, the KE was unpopular, with frequent complaints from tourists regarding the inability to see out ahead. Essentially the "coaches" were no more than service buses without a destination box, but with curtains, and different livery. The KEs were never cascaded onto schools work, unlike almost every other class of service/express bus/coach. All were withdrawn by 1996.

The liveries for coach KEs ware not standard either as exemplified by KE29 photographed at the UITP Conference in the RDS in May 1981. The arrival of the CVH class of Van Hool Acrons in 1986 signalled the end of the KEs on coach work and all were downgraded to express, and eventually service work.

KE41, seen at Busaras in June 1981 carries the more common version of the colour scheme.

Also at the UITP Conference in May 1981, Bombardier unveiled another version of the KE coach, with which it aspired to woo the coaching world. In essence it was the same KE basic shell, in a different colour scheme and with plush seats. No orders came for this particular export possibility. 51KZL, as seen here, would later be reregistered 52 RZO and enter the CIÉ fleet in 1982.

KW1, a wheelchair accessible bus designed by FFG was unveiled at the UITP conference in 1981 – International Year of the Disabled, and was available for hire by CIÉ to various groups requiring this service. Based on a Mercedes chassis, the "Telebus" bus saw very little use, and was sold to a disabled group after a short while, ending up with Harris of Santry in the late 1990s.

Immediately after the final KD double decker, KD366, rolled off the production line in the late spring of 1983, General Automotive Corporation (GAC), who at this stage had bought over Bombardier's shares in the Irish operation, began construction of the 202-strong KC class. What would become KC14 is seen in Shannon under construction, and is destined for Conyngham Road Garage in Dublin City Services.

KC1, being the prototype designed and built by FFG featured a GM / Allison / Rockwell configuration, as in the majority of KDs. It is seen on Dublin's Parnell Square in February 1983 ready to depart on route 36 to Sillogue in Ballymun. KC1 ran on routes 36, 36A, 36B, 70, 76 and 80 alongside C class Leopards until early 1984 when the latter type was finally withdrawn from Dublin City Services. When new it featured a rear destination box, which was quickly dispensed with on entering service from Conyngham Road Garage.

Provincial cities soon received small allocations of KCs for driver familiarisation. KC2, allocated to Cork is seen at Parnell Place was the only one of its class built by Bombardier prior to the changeover to GAC. It was transferred to Phibsboro Garage in Dublin City Services in the Autumn of 1988, and ended its days in 1997 operating out of Summerhill Garage.

Waterford received KC6 and it is photographed in 1983 at the bus station when a few weeks old alongside C5.

The early production KCs entered service in provincial garages - KC3, new to Limerick and then Clontarf in Dublin City Services, KC5/6 in Waterford, KC7/8 in Galway and KC2/9 in Cork. KC7 entered service in September 1983, and was joined by KC101-108 in 1984. In 1989 the bus became an all-over-advert for Denny's, similar to that applied to DF785 in Donnybrook, and was withdrawn in 1999 never making it to schools work.

KC55 crosses the River Dodder on Londonbridge Road in Sandymount towards the last months of route 52 in the summer of 1985. In 1986 the route was to be reconstituted as a DART rail feeder service to UCD's Belfield complex.

KC137 to KC139 were temporarily allocated to Drogheda in 1984/5 to cover vehicle shortages on routes to the popular sea-side villages of Laytown, Bettystown and Clogher Head, from where KC138 had just arrived. They would later be allocated to Clontarf. KC122 and KC123 were also allocated to Dundalk at this time. KCS138 ran as a school bus in Tralee Co. Kerry until 2002.

Cork also received KC 141 which is photographed at Parnell Place Bus Station prior to heading to Macroom in March 1985. The bus spent all its working life in Cork, mainly on city services.

GAC did get to kit assemble some MAN coaches for the Los Angeles Olympics in 1984 one of which is pictured under construction. Though not a CIÉ vehicle, it is a tantalizing taste of what might have been a possibility for the company's coaching requirements.

Prototype bus KR1 photographed at Busaras in Dublin in May 1985. It was one of two rural buses designed by FFG in 1982, KR1, with a DAF engine and the second, KS2, with a Mercedes unit.

KS2, with a Mercedes unit which is photographed en route to Ashbourne in the summer of 1984. Production models would all carry DAF units, with one exception. In 1985, a Cummins engined example, C 529 XEF, was built for demonstration with United Automobile Services in Darlington, and, not finding favour with the operator, was incorporated into the CIÉ fleet in 1987 as KR226. *Photo by Vivian Mangan.*

A typical scene in many locations in Ireland in the mid 1980s would be the KR parked at a railway station, in this case KR195, in Waterford photographed in November 1986. *Photo by Vivian Mangan.*

KR203-225 were "in build" when GAC ceased production in Shannon and went into liquidation in 1986. They were completed by CIÉ later that year and never carried GAC badges front or rear. Those that were taxed in 1986 retained their XZV registration plates. In 1987, a new, simplified, registration system was introduced in the Republic of Ireland, and vehicles presented after 1/1/87 received 87 D plates. KR219 received registration 87 D 2219 under the new vehicle licensing system. *Photo by Vivian Mangan*